I0616628

Lacandon Jungle Press Presents: Build Your Story
A Young Writer's Guide to Storytelling
Flaco Sol

Lacandon Jungle Press

First Edition

Lacandon Jungle Press
www.LJPBooks.com

This book is a work of nonfiction written for young creators. Any resemblance to real people or events is purely coincidental.

ISBN: Paperback – 978-1-967354-09-2 eBook – 978-1-967354-10-8
Cover and interior design by Lacandon Jungle Press

CONTENTS

Getting
Started

Before you jump into the chapters, here is how this guide works.

Each chapter teaches one part of storytelling. You will read the section, learn the idea, and see how it applies to any story you want to write. At the end of every chapter, you will find a page with a simple instruction. This is your practice page.

Instead of writing directly in the book, use a computer, notebook, or separate sheets of paper. That way you can repeat the exercises as many times as you want. Stories change each time you try something new, and you may want to build more than one idea as you grow as a writer.

Think of this guide as a set of tools. You learn one tool at a time. Then you try it. The more you practice, the faster each step will feel. By the end, you will have everything you need to outline a story, plan your scenes, shape your world, and start writing with confidence.

Do not rush. Take your time with each part. You can return to any chapter whenever you need to rebuild something or find your direction again.

When you are ready, turn the page and begin. Your story starts the moment you decide to build it. By the end, you'll have an amazing story, told straight from your heart. You've got this!

YOUR BIG IDEA
How to Catch the Spark That Starts Your Story

E very story begins the same way. Something tiny inside your mind stirs, the way a bright creature might rustle the leaves deep in the Lacandon Jungle. You catch a glimpse. A color. A motion. A feeling. It never shows its full shape at first. It only asks you to follow.

Maybe you picture a kid who finds a hidden path that was not there yesterday. Maybe you imagine a frog who keeps a journal because he has too many secrets to remember. Maybe you see a floating city built in the branches of a single giant tree.

The idea may look unusual. Good. The Jungle never grows anything ordinary.

You do not need a full plan. You do not need a big chart. You only need the spark that refuses to leave you alone. Your job is to catch it long enough to see its outline, the same way you might follow a firefly through the dusk.

To do that, answer three questions. Keep your answers simple and honest.

Who is your hero? Write one or two sentences about the person or creature your story follows. It can be a kid or a tiger or a robot or a shy explorer who wishes they were braver. Do not worry about long descriptions. The Jungle reveals details as you travel.

What are they trying to do? This direction becomes what I call the Heart Trail. It is the path your hero wants to walk, the thing they hope to reach. Maybe they want to find something important or fix a mistake or help someone or discover the truth about a mystery. Pick the goal that pulls them forward.

What is standing in their way? No trail stays clear forever. Something blocks it. I call this the Stone in the Road. It might be a villain or a rule or a fear or a hard choice. It might be something they caused themselves. Whatever it is, your hero must face it before they can reach the end of their Heart Trail.

Now take your answers and fit them into a single paragraph. Do not worry about sounding perfect. Just collect the truth of your idea in one place.

This is what I call your Story Seed.

A Story Seed is small, but it has a way of growing the moment you plant it. If you ever lose your way, read it again. It will remind you where the story wants to go.

Do not panic if your idea looks messy or strange. Many Jungle plants begin twisted or knotted before they reveal their real shape. Stories behave the same way.

Pause for a moment and look at the seed you just made. You did not wait for a perfect idea or a perfect mood. You reached into the green shadows and pulled something alive into the light.

Once a seed touches the soil, it already knows how to become more.

Your story is ready to grow. The Jungle is listening.

PLANT YOUR SEED

Write your own Story Seed in one clear paragraph using your hero, their goal, and what stands in their way.

MEET YOUR HERO

Shaping the Character Who Will Lead the Journey

Now that you have your Story Seed, it is time to meet the one who will carry it through the Jungle. Your hero. Not the kind on posters with perfect hair. The real kind. The kind whose shoelaces get tangled or whose backpack never quite closes or whose courage sometimes hides under a leaf.

Kids often think they need to build a hero the way adults build tax forms. Lines to fill in. Boxes to check. Information nobody actually cares about. Do not do that. You are not building paperwork. You are building a friend who wants to go on a journey with you.

A good hero is someone you want to follow. Someone who has a reason to move. Someone who feels just a little alive even before the story begins.

Here is how to shape that hero without getting lost in the undergrowth.

1. What your hero really wants

Every hero has a want. I call this their Inner Lantern because it glows inside them and lights their way. It might burn brightly or it might flicker, but it is there.

Maybe your hero wants to return something they lost. Maybe they want to make a friend. Maybe they want to prove they are brave. Maybe they want to go home. Maybe they want to explore something forbidden.

Do not try to pick the perfect want. Pick the honest one. This Inner Lantern will guide them the whole way.

2. What makes your hero scared

Every hero fears something. Even the boldest explorers in the Lacandon Jungle feel their stomach twist sometimes. Fear is not a weakness. Fear gives your hero something to overcome.

This is what I call the Shadow Knot. It is the fear or belief that ties your hero up inside.

Maybe your hero is scared of being alone. Maybe they fear failing. Maybe they fear being laughed at. Maybe they fear letting someone down. Maybe they fear what they might discover about themselves.

Do not hide this fear. A Shadow Knot makes your hero human, even if they are a frog with a backpack and big ideas.

3. One thing your hero needs to learn

Heroes begin stories incomplete. That is not a flaw. That is the reason stories exist. Something inside them has to grow or change by the end. This lesson becomes their Growing Vine.

It might be learning to trust someone. It might be learning to speak up. It might be learning to slow down. It might be learning to forgive. It might be learning that mistakes can be fixed.

The Growing Vine is the part of your hero that will reach upward toward the light as the story moves forward.

4. One thing your hero already does well

A hero also needs a strength. Something they carry proudly or quietly. This strength becomes their Bright Skill.

Maybe your hero can solve puzzles. Maybe they can make people laugh. Maybe they listen well. Maybe they climb better than anyone their age. Maybe they know every bird song in the Jungle.

The Bright Skill does not need to save the world. It simply reminds your hero that they are not starting from nothing.

5. Putting it all together

Once you know these four things, write them out in a simple paragraph. Not a chart. Not a form. A paragraph written the way you would describe a friend you care about.

You now have a hero with an Inner Lantern, a Shadow Knot, a Growing Vine, and a Bright Skill. These four pieces create someone who feels real. Someone who can surprise you. Someone who will face the Stone in the Road on their Heart Trail with more than just luck.

6. Do not make them perfect

Perfect heroes are boring. Perfect heroes never learn. Perfect heroes never cry, never laugh at the wrong moment, never make a wrong turn, never spill their soup, never run from something they should face.

Let your hero be a little messy. The Lacandon Jungle is full of mud, and so are the best stories.

7. Meet them with respect

Treat your hero gently. They are not a toy for you to push around. They are a partner. You tell their story, but they carry the weight of it. If you listen closely, you will sometimes hear your hero tell you what they want to do next. When that happens, follow them. They know more than you think.

Take a moment. Read your paragraph out loud. Picture your hero stepping between the trees with their Inner Lantern glowing softly. Picture their Shadow Knot tugging at them. Picture their Bright Skill shining when the path gets dark. Picture their Growing Vine ready to climb.

You know them now.

The story can truly begin.

MEET YOUR GUIDE ON THE TRAIL

Describe your hero in three sentences that show what they want, what scares them, and what they already do well.

The Story Path

Understanding the Eight Beats Every Adventure Follows

E very adventure follows a path, even the wild ones that twist through the Lacandon Jungle where vines grow sideways and the trees whisper their own opinions. Your hero walks this path step by step. You do not need to control every detail. You only need to understand the rhythm.

Here are the eight beats of a story. Think of them as stepping stones that appear one at a time beneath your hero's feet. Each one gives your story direction and shape without turning it into homework.

Picture these clearly. Picture them the way you might picture a hidden trail lit by fireflies.

1. Normal Day

This is your hero's life before anything unusual happens. A quiet moment at the start of the path. A kid eating breakfast. A frog scribbling in his secret journal. A robot sweeping dust from the same corner every morning.

Show the world as it is. Calm. Ordinary. Predictable. This gives the rest of the story contrast. The Lacandon Jungle looks wild only because the village outside it is tame.

2. Something Changes

Something cracks open in your hero's world. I call this the First Drumbeat. It might be strange or scary or wonderful or confusing. It might be small, like a misplaced key, or enormous, like a storm that should not exist.

This change tells your hero that the Normal Day is ending. It tells the reader that the Heart Trail is about to appear.

3. The Big Choice

Your hero decides to go. They step toward the unknown. They say yes to the adventure, even if their Shadow Knot tugs at them. This moment matters because it shows your hero chooses the path instead of being shoved onto it.

Maybe they choose to enter the Jungle. Maybe they choose to help someone. Maybe they choose to chase a mystery. Whatever the choice is, it becomes their first act of courage.

4. Early Challenges

Now the trail begins to twist. Your hero faces small obstacles. These are First Hurdles, the kind that reveal a Bright Skill or deepen a Shadow Knot.

Maybe your hero gets lost. Maybe they meet someone they do not trust yet. Maybe they make a mistake that complicates everything.

These challenges warm the story up. They teach the hero and the reader what kind of journey this will be.

5. The Giant Middle Surprise

Halfway through the story, something major happens. A twist. A discovery. A secret revealed. This is the Great Turning Leaf. It flips the story over and shows something new on the other side.

Maybe a friend is not who they said they were. Maybe the treasure is not where the map pointed. Maybe the real problem is bigger or smaller than anyone thought. Maybe your hero learns something about themselves they were not ready for.

The Giant Middle Surprise changes the direction of the Heart Trail and forces your hero to see the path with new eyes.

6. Things Get Harder

The stakes rise. The Stone in the Road gets heavier. The challenges are not warmups anymore. They matter now.

Your hero might lose something important. They might fail. They might see the truth of their Shadow Knot more clearly.

This beat is where the Jungle grows darker and the vines feel thicker. But this is also where your hero's Growing Vine begins to climb. Hard moments help heroes grow.

7. The Toughest Moment

Every story has a moment when the hero wants to give up. This moment is the Night River, a place that feels cold and impossible to cross. The water rises. The shadows deepen. The Inner Lantern flickers.

Your hero might feel alone or defeated or foolish. They might believe they cannot finish the journey. This is the emotional center of the story. It shows your hero at their lowest, which makes their final climb meaningful.

8. The Finish Line

Your hero faces the final challenge. The last obstacle. The biggest Stone in the Road. They step forward with whatever strength remains, using the Growing Vine they have nurtured and the Bright Skill they carried from the start.

They do not have to win in a perfect way. They only have to face the moment honestly. When the dust settles, your hero is changed. They have walked the Heart

Trail. They have crossed the Night River. They have grown.

Then the world settles into a new shape. It is not the same as the Normal Day. It cannot be. The Jungle changes everyone who walks through it.

Using the Beats

You do not need to outline every beat with absolute precision. You only need to know the order. Let the story move like a river. Let the beats appear when the moment feels right. They will guide your hero through the Lacandon paths and into the light on the other side.

These eight beats are the bones beneath the story's skin. Quiet. Strong. Reliable.

Once you see them, you will always know where the path leads.

MAP THE JOURNEY AHEAD

Fill in your Eight Beats by writing one short sentence for each moment of your story.

SCENES: THE BUILDING BLOCKS

How to Create Moments That Move the Story Forward

A story is not built all at once. You do not roll it out like a carpet. You build it piece by piece, the way someone might build a small shelter in the Lacandon Jungle. A branch here. A vine there. A stone set in the right place.

Each piece is a scene.

Scenes are the moments where things actually happen. They are the steps your hero takes, the conversations that matter, the discoveries that push the Heart Trail forward. If you think of your story as a trail of stepping stones, each stone is a scene. Without them, your hero sinks into the mud and your reader sinks with them.

To keep your scenes strong and clear, use what I call the Four Point Scene Card. Imagine it as a simple card you can hold in your hand, something small enough to tuck in a pocket but powerful enough to guide your entire journey.

Every scene answers four questions. If a moment in your story does not answer these, it might not be a scene at all. It might just be noise pretending to be important.

Here are the Four Points.

1. What is happening?

This sounds simple, but it matters. You should be able to describe the action of the scene in one or two sentences. If you cannot, the scene is trying to do too many things at once.

Maybe your hero is crossing a bridge made of living vines. Maybe they are arguing with a friend. Maybe they are following strange footprints. Maybe they are standing in front of a closed door, trying to decide if they should knock.

Do not start writing until you know what is happening. The Jungle respects clarity.

2. Who wants something here?

Every scene needs desire. Someone wants something in that moment. Someone has a purpose. That someone might be your hero, but it could also be another character. Once you know who wants something, you can feel the pulse of the scene.

Maybe your hero wants answers. Maybe a friend wants forgiveness. Maybe a creature wants to trick your hero. Maybe the villain wants to stop the Heart Trail from moving forward.

A scene without desire is like a fire without heat. It looks interesting but it will not keep anyone warm.

3. What goes wrong or right?

Something must shift. This is the scene's Turn, a natural Lacandon rhythm. The moment must tilt one way or the other. If everything stays the same, the scene is just standing still.

Maybe something goes wrong. The bridge snaps. The clues vanish. The secret is not what your hero expected.

Or something goes right. A clue appears. A new ally steps out from the trees. A skill your hero forgot they had becomes useful again.

Whether the moment turns toward trouble or toward hope, the point is that it turns.

4. How does the story change because of it?

This is the most important question of all. Every scene must push the story forward. Something needs to be different after the scene than it was before it began.

Maybe your hero understands something new. Maybe they lose something. Maybe they gain something. Maybe the Heart Trail becomes clearer. Maybe the Stone in the Road becomes heavier. Maybe the Shadow Knot tightens or loosens.

If the story stays exactly the same after the scene ends, then the scene is not a building block. It is a piece of driftwood. Driftwood floats, but it does not help you build a shelter.

Putting the Points Together

When you sit down to write a scene, jot these four things down. You can write them on a card or at the top of your page. They are your compass. They keep your story from wandering off into the tall grass where readers get lost.

A strong scene feels alive. It starts with a purpose, moves toward a turn, and ends with a change. With this rhythm, the Jungle becomes navigable. Even the twisting vines cannot hide the direction for long.

Scenes Bring the Story to Life

Readers do not fall in love with outlines. They fall in love with scenes. They fall in love with the moment your hero makes a brave choice. Or a foolish one. Or a funny one. They fall in love with the surprise hidden under a leaf or the whisper of danger just out of sight.

Scenes are where your hero breathes. Scenes are where the Inner Lantern glows or flickers or sparks into something new.

Use the Four Point Scene Card every time, and your story will never wander. It will move with confidence, one stone at a time, toward whatever waits at the end of the Heart Trail.

Shape a Moment in the Clearing

Create a Four Point Scene Card by answering the four questions for one scene you want to write.

SIDE QUESTS
Using Smaller Adventures to Strengthen the Main Trail

Every big adventure has little adventures hiding inside it. These smaller journeys are called side quests, and kids love them. They add sparks, surprises, detours, friendships, jokes, mysteries, and moments that feel like fireflies drifting just off the main path.

But side quests can also scatter your story if you do not handle them with care. The Lacandon Jungle is full of interesting trails that lead nowhere, and your reader does not want to wander in circles.

The secret is simple. A side quest must serve the story, not distract from it. If it does not help the hero grow or make the main problem bigger, it becomes noise instead of discovery. Whenever you find a noisy idea, you place it gently in what I call the Maybe Later Basket. That basket keeps your story clean while still honoring all your wild thoughts.

Let us look at how a good side quest works.

1. A side quest helps the hero grow

Your hero has a Growing Vine, a part of themselves that needs to stretch and climb as the story moves forward. A side quest that helps the hero grow might challenge that vine, water it, or show the hero how strong it can become.

Maybe your hero helps a stranger even though they are afraid. Maybe they face a small version of the big problem, learning something that will matter later. Maybe they discover a weakness they did not know they had. Maybe they gain courage because something tiny goes right.

Growth does not need to be dramatic. It can be quiet. The hero might learn patience. They might learn to listen. They might learn they are braver than they believed. These moments matter because they prepare the hero for the larger challenges waiting ahead.

2. A side quest makes the main problem bigger

Stories survive by pressure. If your main problem never changes, your hero never has to adapt. A great side quest can make the heart of the story heavier, more tangled, or more urgent.

Maybe the villain learns something about the hero. Maybe a clue gets destroyed. Maybe a friend gets pulled into danger. Maybe your hero makes a mistake that creates a new Stone in the Road.

When a side quest makes the main problem bigger, it tightens the tension and keeps your reader turning pages. It shows that the Jungle is alive and reacting, not just sitting there waiting.

Side quests that do neither

Sometimes you will think of something fun. A joke. A mini adventure. A character who appears just because you wanted to draw them. These ideas feel exciting, but if they do not grow the hero or tighten the story, they belong in the Maybe Later Basket.

This basket is important. It keeps your creative energy flowing without letting your story drown in extra decorations. You can always come back to the basket later. Some ideas become their own stories. Some become better ideas once they have time to settle.

How to check your side quest

Before you write a side quest, ask two questions.

Does this help my hero grow? Does this make the main problem bigger?

If the answer to either question is yes, you are holding a real side quest, something worthy of your story. If the answer is no, the idea goes in the basket.

It is not lost. It is simply waiting.

Side quests can reveal new parts of the world

Side quests are also useful for worldbuilding. They show corners of the Jungle your hero would not see otherwise. The trading market hidden beneath the roots of an old tree. The river that glows blue when the moon rises. The village of flying turtles that only appears at dawn.

These moments add richness. They make your world feel alive. As long as the side quest also grows the hero or increases the tension, your reader will welcome the detour.

Side quests shape relationships

Friendships, arguments, promises, rivalries, and surprising alliances often take place inside side quests. These smaller journeys give characters space to breathe and learn from each other.

Maybe the hero learns to trust someone new. Maybe they argue with a friend and must repair the bond. Maybe they meet someone who offers guidance. Maybe they discover someone they should avoid.

Side quests let characters become real.

Keep the path clear

A good story feels like a walk through the Jungle with clear markers on the trees. The Heart Trail must always be visible. Side quests are like little arches of flowers you pass beneath. Beautiful, memorable, but never blocking the way.

Use them sparingly. Use them wisely. Use them with purpose.

When in doubt, the Maybe Later Basket waits patiently.

A story with too many side quests becomes tangled. A story with the right ones becomes unforgettable.

Choose a Path Beside the Path

Write one sentence that describes a side quest that helps your hero grow or makes the main problem tougher.

BUILDING YOUR WORLD

Designing the Rules, Wonders, and Details of Your Setting

K ids love worldbuilding. They love drawing maps, naming places, inventing creatures, designing symbols, listing foods, building kingdoms, and imagining strange skies with glowing moons. Their excitement is powerful and wonderful, but it can also spill over like a bucket of paint knocked off a table.

Worldbuilding should feel like decorating a room. You open the windows. You paint the walls. You put a few important things where they belong. You do not need to build a skyscraper with elevators and blueprints and complicated wiring. You just need a space where your story can breathe.

Think of your world the way you think of the Lacandon Jungle. It is big and beautiful and full of secrets, but you only need to show the parts your hero walks through. The rest stays in the shadows until the right moment.

Here are the essentials.

1. What is different about your world

Start with the differences. Readers notice those first. If your world is almost like ours but with one twist, you only need to shine a light on that twist.

Maybe animals talk. Maybe dreams spill into real life. Maybe the weather has feelings. Maybe every child gets a lantern that glows brighter when they learn something new. Maybe the Jungle hums songs only some people can hear.

Do not write everything that is different. Choose the pieces that matter to the story, the parts the hero cannot avoid. If your hero never climbs a mountain, you do not need to describe every mountain range. Let the world open only the doors your hero will walk through.

2. What are the rules

Every world has rules. Even magical ones. Maybe especially magical ones. Rules keep your story honest. Without them, anything can happen, and if anything can happen, nothing feels important.

Think of the rules as the Bones of the World. Quiet and strong beneath everything else.

Maybe magic is powered by memories. Maybe creatures can only speak at sunrise. Maybe travelers must never pick flowers in a certain grove. Maybe crossing a river always changes something about you, even if you cannot see it yet.

Rules make your world feel real because they create limits. Limits create tension. Tension creates story. Rules also prevent your hero from solving problems too easily. If anything could fix the situation, then nothing feels earned.

Choose your rules carefully. Write down only the ones that matter. A world can have many secrets, but your story only needs a few solid bones.

3. What would surprise a visitor

This is my favorite question. Imagine someone from your world visiting ours. They would be surprised by something. Now imagine someone from our world stepping into yours. What detail would catch their breath?

This detail becomes your Wonder Point, a tiny spark that shows how your world thinks differently.

Maybe every insect glows softly at night. Maybe shadows do not match the shape of the person casting them. Maybe plants whisper opinions when you walk past. Maybe everyone wears bells on their shoes so the Jungle knows who is coming.

The Wonder Point should be small but powerful. It makes your world unique without drowning your reader in information.

Let the hero discover the world naturally

Do not dump every detail at once. Let your hero learn about the world piece by piece, the way someone learns a new house by exploring each room. When they taste a fruit, describe it. When they cross a river, show what makes that river special. When they meet a creature, reveal what that creature can do.

The world should reveal itself through the story, not before it.

Use the world to shape the story

A good world is not a backdrop. It has a personality. It encourages some things and makes other things difficult. It supports the hero or challenges them.

If the world has floating islands, your hero might fall or fly. If the world has strict rules about magic, your hero might break one. If the Jungle itself has moods, your hero might need to earn its trust.

Let the world push and pull the story. Let it matter.

Keep your notes simple

Kids often want to create entire encyclopedias. Entire species lists. Entire histories. Entire calendars. That is wonderful, but it is easy to drown in the details and forget the actual story.

Encourage yourself to write only what you need for now. You can always expand later. Let your world grow like a garden. Plant what matters. Trim what gets in the way. Allow new ideas to bloom when the story asks for them.

Your world does not need to be perfect

Jungle paths bend. Rivers twist. Trees grow in strange patterns. A world does not need to follow perfect logic. It only needs to follow its own logic.

Build the parts your hero touches. Let the rest remain in the shadows. If you ever need to shine a light deeper into the world, it will be waiting.

A story with a well built world feels like a place you could step into. A place with edges you can touch. A place where every sound hints at something more.

Build only what matters, and your world will feel alive.

Build the World Around You

Choose one detail, one rule, and one surprise that define your story world and write a sentence about each.

detail   rule   surprise

YOUR STORY ON ONE PAGE

Simplifying Your Whole Idea Into a Guide You Can Use

There is a moment in every adventure when you need a map. Not a giant scroll that takes ten people to unroll. Not a complicated chart full of symbols nobody understands. You need something small. Something you can fold into your pocket. Something you can pull out whenever the Jungle gets too thick to see ahead.

This is where the **One Page Blueprint** comes in.

A single sheet. One page. Everything important about your story gathered in one place. When you look at it, you should feel like you are holding the blueprint of a secret hideout. A place only you know how to enter.

Here is how to build it.

1. Start with your Story Seed

Copy your Story Seed right at the top of the page. Do not rewrite it. Do not decorate it. Do not try to make it fancy. Keep it exactly as you first wrote it.

Your Story Seed is the core of everything. It reminds you what your hero wants, what stands in their way, and why the journey matters. When you feel lost, this line at the top of your page will call you back like a soft drumbeat.

2. Add the 8 Beats

Next, write out the eight beats of your story. Only a few words each. You do not need paragraphs here. Just a clear signpost for each moment.

Normal Day Something Changes The Big Choice Early Challenges The Giant Middle Surprise Things Get Harder The Toughest Moment The Finish Line

These are your stepping stones. Your hero will move across them one by one. Writing them on your One Page Blueprint makes them feel solid under your feet.

3. Make a list of your characters

Do not list every possible character. Only the ones who matter. Your hero. A friend. A guide. A rival. A villain. A creature who plays an important part. Write their names or descriptions in a simple list.

Give each one a few words. Enough to remind you of their Inner Lantern or their Shadow Knot or the reason they matter in the story. This list keeps your cast clear in your mind, the same way a traveler keeps track of companions on a long journey.

4. Write down the world rules

Remember the Bones of the World. The rules that keep your world honest. Write only the rules that matter for the story. If magic fades at sunset, write that. If certain creatures cannot lie, write that. If crossing a river changes you, write that.

A few rules are all you need. They will shape every chapter. They will also stop you from breaking your world by accident as you write.

5. Choose three favorite moments

This part is important. Pick three moments you cannot wait to write. They might be big or small. They might be loud or quiet.

Maybe it is the moment your hero meets the creature in the glowing cave. Maybe it is the argument that changes everything. Maybe it is the moment your hero almost gives up. Maybe it is the moment the Bright Skill finally shines.

When you write these three moments on your One Page Blueprint, you give yourself something to look forward to. These are your **Lantern Scenes**, moments that pull you through the Jungle even when the path gets muddy.

6. Keep the page simple

Your One Page Blueprint should not feel crowded. It should feel like a doorway. The clearer the page, the easier it is to use.

If the page feels messy, take a breath and rewrite it. Not the story. Just the page. Clean and simple. Your entire journey on one sheet of paper.

7. Why this works

Writers think they need thousands of notes before they begin. But most of those notes gather dust. What you need is focus. A compass. A blueprint that fits in your hand.

The One Page Blueprint keeps you from drowning in your own ideas. It shows you the Hero, the Path, the World, and the Lantern Scenes all at once. When you start writing, you can glance at the page and feel confident again.

Your story becomes a structure you understand, not a maze you stumble through.

8. Carry it with you

Fold the blueprint. Put it next to your notebook. Tape it to the wall. Slip it into a book. This page belongs to you. It will travel with your hero from the first step of the Heart Trail to the end of the journey.

Whenever you feel unsure, unfold it. Look at the Story Seed. Look at the 8 Beats. Look at your characters and the world rules and the Lantern Scenes waiting for you. The page will remind you that you already know where the story is going.

You built the hideout. You built the map. You know the way.

GATHER EVERYTHING ON ONE PAGE

Create your one page plan by listing your Story Seed, your Eight Beats, your characters, your world rules, and your three favorite moments.

Fix-It Station
Quick Repairs for Boring Middles, Flat Heroes, and Stuck Ideas

Every storyteller reaches a moment when the trail gets messy. The vines get thicker. The map feels wrong. The words run away and hide behind trees. This happens to everyone. Even grown writers. Even writers who pretend it never happens to them.

That is why your story needs a Fix It Station, a tiny repair shop you can visit whenever something feels wobbly or broken. Think of it as a bright little hut deep in the Lacandon Jungle. There is a roof made of wide leaves. There are tools hanging on the walls. There is a workbench where you can place any part of your story and figure out what it needs.

Let us walk inside and look at the tools.

1. The Middle Is Boring

This is the most common problem in all storytelling. The middle of a story is like a long stretch of Jungle path. If nothing changes, your reader starts staring at their shoes.

When your middle gets dull, you need a spark. Here are three fast sparks.

Add a surprise. Something unexpected appears. A clue. A creature. A mistake. A new rule of the world. A twist that makes the reader lean forward.

Add a discovery. Your hero learns something important. A secret. A warning. A truth they were not ready for.

Add a mistake. Your hero does something wrong. Maybe they trust the wrong person. Maybe they break something valuable. Mistakes keep stories alive because they force the hero to react.

Any one of these will wake the middle of your story like thunder in the canopy.

2. Your Hero Feels Flat

A flat hero is like a puppet with its strings cut. They move, but nothing feels real.

To fix a flat hero, open the little drawer labeled Heart Tools. Inside are two questions.

What is your hero afraid of? What is your hero hiding?

Give your hero a fear or a secret. Even a small one. A fear of letting someone down. A secret they have never told a friend. A doubt they cannot shake. These are Shadow Knots, and they make your hero human.

Once you know what your hero fears or hides, scenes suddenly have weight. Choices matter. Emotions matter. Readers care.

3. Nothing Is Happening

If your story feels like it is standing still, then your stakes are too low. Stakes are the reason your story matters. They are the reason your hero cannot just go home and eat a sandwich.

To fix quiet stakes, use the Pressure Pump.

Make something important harder. Make the problem deeper. Make the cost of failure clearer. Make the Stone in the Road heavier.

If your hero loses something when they fail, readers will pay attention. If nothing is at risk, the story feels like a walk instead of a journey.

Pressure creates motion.

4. You Are Stuck

Every writer gets stuck. Sometimes the path goes dark. Sometimes you feel like sitting on a log and waiting for inspiration to carry you. But inspiration is lazy. It rarely shows up when you call it.

When you are stuck, use the Jump Ahead Lever.

Pick a moment you are excited to write. A big moment. A secret moment. A funny moment. A dramatic moment. Any moment that sparks your curiosity.

Skip straight to that moment and write it.

You do not need to write scenes in order. Stories are not chains. They are living creatures, and you can start shaping them from any angle. When you write the scene you are excited about, the energy returns. The path brightens. The earlier scenes often reveal themselves once the destination is clearer.

5. The Scene Feels Useless

Sometimes a scene just sits there like a stone you tripped on. To fix it, pull out your Four Point Scene Card and test it.

What is happening? Who wants something here? What goes wrong or right? How does the story change?

If your scene fails these questions, it is not broken. It is simply unnecessary. Move it to the Maybe Later Basket and let the story breathe.

6. The Dialogue Feels Like Filler

If your characters are talking without purpose, give someone in the scene a goal and someone else an obstacle. Do this and the conversation will move like a stream instead of a puddle.

7. The Ending Feels Weak

A weak ending usually means the hero did not change enough. Look back at their Growing Vine. Did they really learn the lesson you planned? If not, adjust the final challenge so it tests that lesson clearly.

8. Do Not Be Afraid to Cut

Writers sometimes cling to lines they like, even when those lines do nothing for the story. Cutting a scene or sentence does not hurt the story. It frees it.

Think of pruning vines. When you cut one branch, another gets more sunlight.

The Fix It Station is always open

There is no wrong time to visit. No mistake too small or too big. Stories bend. Stories twist. Stories sometimes break. The magic is that they can always be repaired.

You are not alone in the Jungle. You have tools now. Use them whenever you need to.

Repair a Broken Step

Choose one part of your story and fix it by adding a surprise, a fear, a higher stake, or a clearer goal.

Time to Build
How to Begin Writing With Confidence and Momentum

There comes a moment in every journey when you stop planning and start moving. You have gathered your tools. You have learned the path. You have shaped your hero and planted your Story Seed. You have built your One Page Blueprint and stocked your Fix It Station. You know the Heart Trail. You know the Stone in the Road. You know the shape of the world your story breathes in.

Now it is time to step forward.

This is the part where many young writers hesitate. They stand at the edge of the trail, staring into the trees, wondering if they are ready. They think they need one more idea, one more outline, one more practice run. But stories do not grow from waiting. Stories grow from motion.

You have the map. Start walking.

Your hero cannot take a single step until you guide them. They are standing there, Inner Lantern glowing softly, Shadow Knot tugging at their heart, Bright Skill ready to help them, Growing Vine eager to stretch. They are looking at you. They are waiting.

Heroes need someone to move their legs.

Writing the first sentence may feel like stepping onto a rope bridge that hangs above a long drop, but here is the truth. You do not need to see the whole bridge to take the first step. The plank beneath your foot is enough. Then the next one. Then the next.

Your story will reveal itself the way the Lacandon Jungle reveals trails. Slowly at first. Then suddenly. Then all at once, like something alive that is glad you finally arrived.

Do not expect perfection. Perfection is a ghost. It shows up only after the story exists, not before. Write a messy beginning. Write a confused middle. Write a brilliant moment in the wrong place. Write scenes out of order if you have to. None of that matters. What matters is motion.

Once you begin, something amazing happens. Your hero starts to speak. They make choices you did not plan. They find allies you did not expect. They lead you toward scenes you did not know were waiting. This is the magic of storytelling. You build the world, and then the world surprises you.

If you get stuck, you already know what to do. Visit the Fix It Station. Turn the Pressure Pump. Check your Four Point Scene Card. Glance at your One Page Blueprint. Skip ahead to a Lantern Scene that excites you. Shake the branches until an idea drops.

You have tools now. You are not wandering blind.

Some writers think they need permission to start. As if someone must tap them on the shoulder and tell them they are allowed to create something new. That is not true. If you have an idea that pulls you forward, that is permission enough.

Your story belongs to you. It waits in the trees, ready to become real the moment you choose to begin.

Sit down. Open your notebook. Place your hands where they need to be. Take a breath. Then write a sentence. Any sentence. It does not need to be beautiful. It only needs to be honest.

Once that first sentence exists, the second one is easier. Then the third. Soon you will forget you were ever afraid to begin. You will be too busy walking the Heart Trail with your hero beside you.

Writing is not magic. Writing is momentum. One step. One scene. One problem. One surprise. You already know how to build each of those things. You have practiced them. You have studied them. You have shaped them into tools.

Now use them.

Stories do not write themselves. They are built by explorers who step into the unknown even when the trees look tall and the shadows feel deep. Explorers like you.

You have everything you need. You are ready. The Jungle is waiting. Your hero is waiting. The page is waiting.

It is time to build.

Take Your First Step Into the Jungle

Write the first paragraph of your story using everything you built in this guide.

Glossary of Lacandon Jungle Press Vocabulary

Story Seed
The small idea that begins your story. A short paragraph that captures your hero, their goal, and the obstacle they face.

Heart Trail
The main goal your hero wants to reach. It is the direction of their journey.

Stone in the Road
The obstacle blocking your hero's Heart Trail. It can be a problem, a fear, or a hard choice.

Inner Lantern
Your hero's natural strength. It is something they already do well before the story begins.

Eight Beats
A simple map of story events from beginning to end.

Four Point Scene Card
A guide for shaping a single scene.
It answers four questions:
What is happening
Who wants something
What goes right or wrong
How does the story change

Side Quest
A smaller story that helps the hero grow or makes the main problem larger.

World Rules

The guidelines that make your story world feel real and understandable.

Three Moments

Three scenes or images you are excited to write. They help you stay motivated.

Fix It Station

A set of quick tools that help you solve common story problems.

First Drumbeat

The moment your story truly begins. It is the first clear action, choice, or change that starts the hero on their path.

Jungle Map Page

A single page that holds your Story Seed, your Eight Beats, your characters, your world rules, and your three favorite moments.

A Note From Flaco Sol

Building a story is not about talent or luck. It is about curiosity. If you can wonder, you can write. If you can picture a hero standing at the edge of something unknown, you can guide them across it.

Keep your One Page Blueprint nearby. Visit your Fix It Station whenever you need to. Trust your Inner Lantern. It always knows where to shine.

The Lacandon Jungle will always have another trail. Whenever you feel ready, come back and explore more.

TRY THIS NEXT

You have reached the end of the guide, but not the end of your work. You now have the tools to begin your own story and the practice pages to help you move forward. The more often you return to these steps, the stronger your writing will become.

If you want to keep sharpening your storyteller muscles, here are a few simple activities you can use anytime.

Write a moment from your hero's past.
Choose a memory that shaped them. Something small that still matters.

Add a new rule to your world and test it.
Write a short scene where this rule changes what a character can or cannot do.

Draw a simple map of your story.
It does not need to be perfect. Let it be quick and messy, the kind explorers sketch in the field.

Create a small side quest.
Decide if it helps your hero grow or makes the main problem larger. If it does neither, place it in the Maybe Later Basket.

Write the scene you are avoiding.
Difficult scenes often reveal something important, both to the reader and to you.

Use these activities whenever you feel stuck or whenever you want to start a new idea. Your skills grow each time you practice, and the guide is here for you whenever you choose to return to it.

Now begin your story. The rest of the path belongs to you.

ABOUT THE AUTHOR

Flaco Sol is a storyteller who believes every kid carries a spark inside them. Some sparks whisper. Some sparks shout. All of them deserve space to grow. He writes books that help young creators build worlds, shape heroes, and follow the Heart Trail of their imagination.

He is the author of the *Tico Goes to School* books, including the English, Spanish, and Indonesian editions. His stories travel across languages and cultures, reaching young readers wherever their curiosity leads them.

Build Your Story is his guide for kids who want to create their own adventures. Whether you are dreaming up a frog with a backpack or a robot who collects memories, Flaco Sol is here to help you bring that idea to life.

More Lacandon Jungle Press titles are on the way. The Jungle always has another trail.

THANK YOU FOR READING

Readers help stories grow. If you enjoyed this guide and want to help other young creators discover it, consider leaving a kind review on Amazon or your favorite bookstore site. It helps the Jungle reach new explorers.

And if you ever begin a story using the tools in this book, know that I am cheering for you from the clearing just beyond the trees.